At one point in Sally Ashton's new book, *The Behaviour of Clocks*, the speaker says, *I testify to what I saw*. It is by meticulously bearing witness to events throughout the book that the speaker is able to celebrate and transcend the mutability of Time, referenced in the title. In this sense, Ashton's real and imagined travelogue hearkens back to Jean Follain's classic, *A World Rich in Anniversaries*, while also becoming on its own one of the most engaging books of prose poetry I've read in the last ten years.

—PETER JOHNSON, author of *Eduardo and "I"*

Ashton's investigative meditations maintain constant awareness of territories shared by physics and poetry. These wonderfully reflective poems arise from something like a physicist's precision of mind and a shaman's sensitivity of vision. Wistful, fluent, and beautiful, the book launches inquiries into time, being, motion, and travel. Ashton gives us a poetry and a physics that probe powerful unseen forces. She shows us how both practices manifest as acute attention to and curiosity about the world. An expanded sense of *terroir* pervades these poems. This unfolds as a poetics of place not limited to wine and vineyards, but rather enlarged to address an emotional and spiritual sense of grateful, yet tenuous located-ness on our fragile planet.

—AMY GERSTLER, author of *Scattered at Sea*

Poems are magical because they operate both inside and outside of time. Sally Ashton's ambitious and marvelous *The Behaviour of Clocks* uses Albert Einstein's unusually poetic theories of time as points of departure to travel across and through time, countries, concepts, and characters. She brilliantly marries the narrative of prose with the lyricism of poetry to create a series of hybrid texts that echo Charles Baudelaire, Gertrude Stein, Francis Ponge, and Mary Ruefle. Her poems take us to Italy, to the past, and to the moon, but also to those vast continents of the imagination where *wherever we wander we're home*. Dear Weary Traveler, I have good news. You can at last sit back and relax. Make yourself comfortable because you will not want to leave this book.

—DEAN RADER, author of *Self-Portrait as Wikipedia Entry*

In *The Behaviour of Clocks*, Sally Ashton's poems move like foreign landscapes, strange and luminous as the *wind pressed against blades of grasses*. Invoking DaVinci, Einstein, Whitman, Pessoa, time is a radiant prism in her deft hand—elliptical, backward, stilled, and spun off the wheel of the ordinary altogether. Reaching toward history as vigorously as a *glossary of tomorrows*, her riveting inquiry loosens time from its linear track. If Ashton *brings home the r⸺⸺ ⸺⸺ out*, then we are gifted the chance to dwell in all the *possible c*

—JENNIFER K. SWEENEY, author of *How to Live*

THE BEHAVIOUR OF CLOCKS

THE BEHAVIOUR OF CLOCKS

POEMS

SALLY ASHTON

WordFarm
SEATTLE, WASHINGTON

WordFarm
334 Lakeside Ave S, #207
Seattle, WA 98144
www.wordfarm.net
info@wordfarm.net

USA ISBN-13: 978-1-60226-021-4
USA ISBN-10: 1-60226-021-4
Printed in the United States of America
Cover Design: Andrew Craft
First Edition: 2019

Library of Congress Cataloging-in-Publication Data

Names: Ashton, Sally, 1954- author.
Title: The behaviour of clocks / Sally Ashton.
Description: First edition. | Seattle, Washington : WordFarm, 2019.
Identifiers: LCCN 2018055584 (print) | LCCN 2018059166 (ebook)
| ISBN 9781602264281 (ebook) | ISBN 1602264287 (ebook) | ISBN
9781602260214 (pbk.: alk. paper)
Subjects: LCSH: Prose poems, American.
Classification: LCC PS3601.S57 (ebook) | LCC PS3601.S57 A6 2019
(print) | DDC
  811/.6--dc23
LC record available at https://lccn.loc.gov/2018055584

P 10 9 8 7 6 5 4 3 2
Y 24 23 22 21 20 19

for Fionn

Who knows where the time goes?
—SANDY DENNY

CONTENTS

PREFACE

I took the title, *The Behaviour of Clocks*, from the name of a chapter in Albert Einstein's *Relativity: The Special and General Theory*, a book he wrote for the layperson in an attempt to simplify his theories of time, space, and motion, to make them more accessible.

I'm not a scientist. I became interested in Einstein after attending a local conference on creativity where a photograph of him playing a violin appeared on the screen. It struck me immediately. I'd never heard that he often played his violin, Lina, when struggling with complex equations. The speaker talked about the connections between scientific inquiry and artistic practice. I live in the Silicon Valley, birthplace of the tech industry and epicenter of innovation. It was as if I'd just been let into the club. Before long, I was pestering a physicist friend, Stefan Moeller, with questions. He suggested Einstein's book, and off I went, intrigued by possible parallels in these two theoretically oppositional practices. It was Einstein's famous "thought experiments," a series of metaphors involving the movement of trains and clocks, that began to captivate my imagination. Albert became my unwitting muse.

He's not an easy teacher. However, before long I found that inhabiting his thought experiments in my struggle to grasp the spacetime continuum began to frame my own work's inquiry into time—the simultaneity of the past, present, and future in how each informs any moment—and ultimately shaped this book.

Sally Ashton

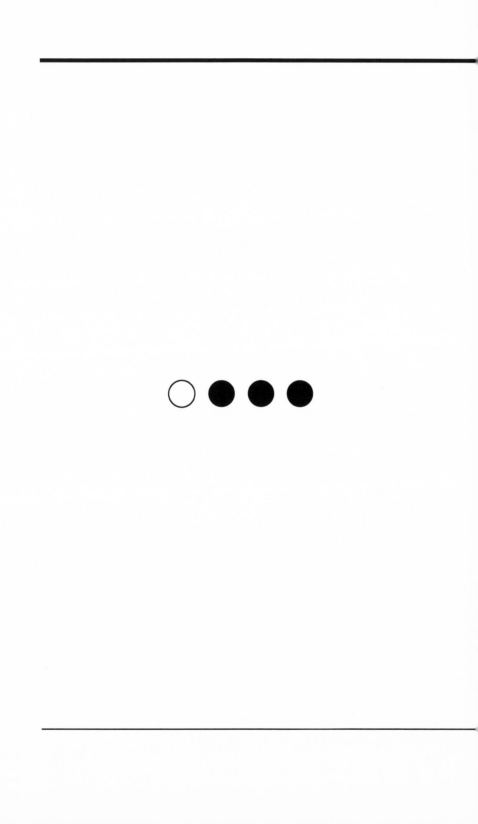

A Theory of Relativity

I stand at the window of a railway carriage.
—ALBERT EINSTEIN

Across from me on a train Albert sat facing backwards, a little table between us, his forehead pressed against the glass. His eyes flickered as if to count passing fence posts. At length he reached a small notebook from a chest pocket, placed it on the table, jotted something down. I tried not to stare but couldn't make out what he wrote even when I did. He smiled. *May I trade seats with you for a while, my dear?* What could I say? In spite of my motion sickness, I agreed. For one thing, the train travelled a relatively straight path, plus his eyes were so kind and sad. He steadied my elbow until I was seated, took his seat, turned again to the window, again to his notes. Then I watched, as he had, the landscape recede, what I knew blurred in immeasurable distance. The sky lost light, Albert's white head bobbed, and just before I slept a luminescent clock appeared in the sky, though now I see it was the moon itself wearing a clock face that watched us speed by, or did we too appear to be standing completely still?

ONE

A ship is a piece of floating space

—MICHEL FOCAULT

You travel by airship—a jet—a placeless place at once threshold
and destination, neither here nor yet there. You fly, translated
to a café table set on uneasy cobble under some broad-leafed
tree, the days turning to memories you will call "Portugal," or
"Italy," or "that summer when." You navigate by train schedule,
by guidebook, by the sidewalk underfoot, and think you could
stay. Traveling itself a placeless place you begin to feel at home
in. You learn to move slow in the afternoons, to count change or
be shortchanged, to say "I don't speak . . ."

Translation, the movement of meaning from one language to
another, connects thought to voice, a floating space between
people. Time, memory, meaning—these spaces by which you
travel.

Airport Malpensa, Milan

In flight the late day gleams red, attendants pass out eye masks,
pull window shades closed, turn off lights. Call it night. It isn't
any hour but a place hurtling over land then water, across clouds
and stars, the misted window, out of day through night and
day again while no time passes but we pass through, rushed to
a future that frames a tilted *now*. The stem of my watch falls off,
disappears somewhere under my feet. No one meets us. We get
our luggage, our passports stamped, trudge outside to the line
of buses waiting in the dark of the next moment already falling
forward.

When We Were in Italy

When we drove across the country, past the fields, past the paper
forests. When we noticed every village was marked by a steeple.
When we mourned each farmhouse tumbled into the cave of
itself. When we knew none could be restored. The sun said this
plainly, its words a glossary of tomorrows it will not be turned
back from. Oats drying in a field. Everywhere a chance to forget.
And one evening from a hillside after dinner, lightning bugs
flicker in an olive orchard. No shooting star, but the wine is very
good.

The Road to Chualar

I testify to what I saw—something aglint in the distance. A
wink. Maybe miracles at work like new houses or springs of
water fountaining forth, the adobe furrows rinsed wet and black.
To the west, the mountains' dark margin held it in, held them
back—fields of gold, a bird turning on silvered wings—*did not our
hearts burn within us?* Shadows fell between the mountains' knees,
and what could ignite did, just like that, spent vines ablaze, the
sky forgotten. Stands of poplars, too, offered a type of forgiveness
to incurious cows. People bowed low among lettuces. It was over
in an instant. The CD ended, the road pulled away so I wouldn't
see the shining dim or night veil what I had seen, what burns
within.

Some Birth Day

Because my soul, open like a tin can under heaven, caught lost
light refracted from a planet or star I never saw but felt illumi-
nate my empty core, the dark matter of fact, and like a can once
opened can never be resealed, this became my because, the thin
curved metal of my remaining days, the lid-off-mouth-open-
catch-all-that-can-be mystery of moment rolled under aluminum
stars, a comet's glance, the knife-blade moon slicing, sliding,
O Moon. And you, Sun, bleached memories of wakefulnesses
flickering empty as a can, complete as a can can be opened, open
empty under heaven, matter's dark fact and the seasons, turning.

Family Album I

*   *   *

A snowstorm, rural Tennessee, 1919. Grandma goes into labor at home two months early. The doctor sets the baby aside; how can it live. The midwife, a cousin, swaddles my dad and lays him in a box surrounded by flannel-wrapped canning jars she's filled with warm water.

*   *   *

As a baby Dad never crawls but scoots on his bottom. Grandma sews one of Grandpa's old banjo heads to the seat of his britches to keep them from wearing out.

*   *   *

Dad's family is seventh-generation Methodist, which means since Creation. The family, Tennessee farmers, supported the Confederates. Dad finds mini balls, bullets, a cannonball, and Civil War uniform buttons, both sides, in the fields where he plays.

*   *   *

Via Sacra

A pilgrim's journey up a worn cobbled path twists through
trees and centuries, polished by faithful feet: the penitents,
the grateful ones, those who sought particular mercy, some
deliverance from pain. Dioramas stand along the way, life-size,
Christ's passion recreated, a donation-only coin box, figures
viewed through glass. Press a button for illumination. Light falls
across veined marble—the shadows of suffering resume.

I continue walking, peering in windows, hoping. I want
something to move.

Side Trip

We hike to a hilltop above the Collio outside Villa Russiz up a
tractor path that steers through the vineyards—dusty, hot,
steep—glad for walking shoes and the breeze that blows cool off
the Adriatic, off the Alps. The two winds meet here, a local says.
A domed mausoleum stands silent among a crown of cypress
and pine that bends and murmurs like the oldest story. We are
quieted and see the lay of the land we've come to, a countryside
whose bloody battles lie healing beneath vineyards, an occasional
stone farmhouse, the spire of some village. It's as if we'd traveled
by horseback or by memory. By the scent of the earth. We nap
there under the rocking branches. We watch the sky.

But life is a busy thing, each ant, a fly buzzing near. A leaf that
turns. Words that won't fill my mouth, my mouth full of
emptiness like wind pressed against blades of grass. The man
who brought us there sits up. *Time is short*, he says, *time is beautiful.*
Our son appears then among the grapevines. One row plowed,
one left to weeds.

Gratitude

The woman woke from her nap. A breeze tossed the greeny branches overhead. Some bird wheedled in a way that matched the motion of the wind, the leaves. A stem of grass teased her bare ankle. The dry air buzzed. In one direction vineyard unfurled, rising, falling with the hills. In the other the steeple and tiled roofs of some small town stood almost asleep. She didn't want to move either. It was good that dinosaurs were extinct. They would have ruined everything.

Jet Lag

Now my canoe glides across a small lagoon. I trail my fingers and watch the ripples fan out behind the boat as long as I can. Already the twists and turns of the journey recede, and the canoe noses toward shore. I don't want to get out. When I look down at the water, a face searching in a wavery mirror peers back. The bow runs aground on the sandy bottom, but I pretend to sleep. My name is called. I answer *I'm sleeping* though nothing comes out of my mouth.

Telling Time

It is not possible to obtain a reasonable definition of time with the aid of clocks.
—ALBERT EINSTEIN

He turns from the window. Across their shared table his companion peers out into the dusk, so intent. So sincere! The way she'd watched him earlier. He settles back in his seat and the train's steady rhythm, closes his eyes. To try. To try and keep it simple. What can he say that won't sound crazy? That clocks run slower in space, that time isn't what it seems?

A town's lights flash past; the train never slows. She sleeps, perhaps dreaming. He opens his notebook. He knows what he'll tell her. He'll tap the glass, point. She'll lean in. *Let's imagine,* he'll begin, *you stand on that embankment watching the train pass, and I drop a stone out the window . . .* he writes long into the night, completely loses track of time.

TWO

Sunday, Leivi

Awakened by church bells to a morning gray and silver, a morning different from all others though morning is always the same. Olive hillsides, mist. Rain chatters on the plastic corrugated cover of the deck outside our room's stone walls in a small overnight town. The narrow road curves against the hillside. Each bend reveals a home, a field, an orchard. Stucco, vine, and always stone, a landscape rolling toward the horizon and the imagined sea. In the town café, locals are gathered over coffee. Their voices drop when we enter. We order coffees, take a table in the back.

Later, the windshield wipers keep their own time. The rain stops, the morning continues, and I understand how "soundless" is different from silence, how rain causes ink to bleed, how I will never be as old as these stones.

Clocks Without Faces

Let someone else tell the time. I can't see it anymore and unlearn its courtesies, begin to dismantle its many faces, crude symbols of the illimitable sphere time really occupies. Its hands do not simply sweep flat circles but travel arcs through all possible circumferences, somewhat how we perceive the second, minute and hour hands to run at separate speeds while on the same level course. Instead, true hands would be seen to gesture both away and toward us at untamed angles and velocities. Bringing us near, drawing us away. The sundial's simplicity proves far more accurate, equating time with light and the movement of shadows, as is an hourglass' passage of sand, random grains pouring from chamber to chamber, or a year marked by a revolution of the whole tipping planet. The way night, like the past, can be measured by dreams, or the present in the flight of a green parrot. So also the future. In this way we would move richly through time without any regulating gears if we could only remember how. And such is childhood's privilege; and such the pleasure and sorrow of old age.

Family Album II

* * *

My Swedish grandmother, Dad's mom, is orphaned in Chicago.
A childless Swedish couple from church takes her in. Grandma
believes they adopt her. They do not; she works as their servant.

* * *

At sixteen, Grandma gets a job with Sears and Roebuck, one of
their first female employees. On the other side of the family, a
great-uncle receives, then sends back, a mail-order bride. Family
members everywhere dream Christmas wishes, put the old Sears
catalogs in their outhouses.

* * *

Grandpa, Dad's daddy, an auctioneer and a circuit judge, rides
the county on his horse, dabbles in real estate. Bankrupt in the
Depression, the family leaves Tennessee for California where
Grandpa has been offered work on a family friend's ranch. Years
later, I am four years old. Grandpa sits me in front of him on his
horse named Dixie, calls me Sassafras.

* * *

Finding Time I

The distinction between past, present and future is only a
stubbornly persistent illusion.
—ALBERT EINSTEIN

Neptune rises from a statuary sea, water streaming from the
nipples of his mermaids' breasts. I walk the city's streets laid out
in spokes from the central piazza, a medieval wheel still turning.
Shaded porticoes shelter me. Faded frescoes arch over my head, a
reason to say *ochre*. Red tiled roofs jumble against each other, and
ancient canals disappear underground before I even know they
are there, lost below the city's modern streets where the Roman
aqueduct still runs. I stand beneath the basilica's vaulted reach
that parses centuries of prayers in motes of dust. Statues torn
by grief gape at the fallen Savior. In the floor, inlaid in brass by
a Renaissance astronomer, a meridian line still marks days and
seasons, precisely measuring time's passage. For no one.

My planet is making me dizzy

satellites skim its surface
beam back the spin lights cloud
day and night flash across my screen
I cannot stand still from the outside in
what about gravity—how long will it
hold they don't even know how it works
don't panic the whole world tilts
mad teacups I never noticed
before YouTube choreographed our
heavenly bodies to music watched
the galaxies near the speed of light startled
stars time dilates I spend my
afternoons holding on nights given to
sleep seasick dreams coiled like
forgotten telephone cord earth rotates
counter-clockwise from the North
clockwise from the South but from the side
my planet is a giant blue and turtle-green
wheel I ride tumbling day to night
the speed of sound desire the speed of light

In the Rain, Udine

(I have seen lizards—brown lizards). Here a man in the court-
yard uses a broom against the asphalt, against the leaves, even as
the gusts of wind blow more down, spatter rain under the eaves
where I sit, drops hitting my neck. From a dry perch somewhere
the cuckoo repeats herself. The day repeats some other day, and
the rain, too, finds a way to discuss its memories, its discoveries.

The brown lizard knows some truth the way he disappears at a
gesture, slides away smooth against the granite wall into a niche
only he can see, only he understands, brown lizard. What is any
object? Which observation bears repeating? Which finds its way
against granite to bask in the sun or skitter to some secret place
at the sound of thunder? Which becomes story? (Now the rain
pours).

No Map

In Bologna we come in from the rain. I don't know what we'll find or how we might live. The city is red, rose, umber. Hills. Sky. Moonlit statues. Rain on cobblestones. We follow porticoes. I take photographs. We sleep in two narrow beds side by side, sailors on night's wide dream. We sleep well. Morning enters through shutters and calls from the streets. I drink black coffee, bright and bitter, like each day is bright and turning to the next. And I turn with them.

Venezia on the Water, Rising

Back out of all this now too much for us.
—ROBERT FROST

The city is as it sounds. Canals, the steps leading into them,
the myth of sinking. I won't restate your memories, share
photographs taken from bridges or diminish what is found there:
concessions, Japanese tour guides holding flags. In the piazza in
the afternoon under an enormous sun, an orchestra plays. We
pay an eight-euro cover charge to sit and listen. A man feeds
pigeons next to the sign that tells him not to. He vanishes in a
cloud of wings.

Einstein's Violin

He tucks it under his chin, raises bow to string, the fingerboard
running straight from cheek into the palm of his cupped left
hand. Cochlea, clavicle, each fingertip curved some for the
balance of the bow, others poised on the strings. So much curled
into the minute before music begins. He cocks an eyebrow
toward the music stand, finds his place in the lines and spaces.
The intervals of sound, like distance and time, paused. He scans
the pattern of notes, the signature, the notation. A specific
gravity. Downbow, and the universe moving in one direction
feels the pull in another. Sound expands, reverberates, notes
improvising some rhapsody, harmonies he hears the way he sees
the nature of energy, vibrating. He taps his foot, keeping time.

After the Statues

After the statues had stood for as long as I could watch them in the piazzas, the cathedrals, the museums, after I had learned to navigate the ancient winding streets by their locations, had seen birds and tourists pose and play on them, after moonlight had glazed pale shoulders and thighs, spears, fins and cherubs, wings, waves and columns spangled as equally as the pavement squares, after I resumed my journey, after miles and years, kingdoms, wars, and centuries of lives passed, passing, and will pass, as mine will pass, I know the statues will be there, as if enchanted, as if time itself could so simply be made to stand still.

Leonardo's Lost Robot

To know the body from the inside out, the wrap of layered
muscle, ligament, tendon strung like cords. To know their feel
and elasticity, their weight. To diagram each joint from any
angle, a mastery of mechanics. Drawings—superior to words—
make incarnate a vision engendered in the soul's eye. How like
a system of cables and counterweights! Sketched by daylight,
by candlelight, the shadows fall this way then that, suggest the
movement that could be. Each midnight interview with a
cadaver yields insight. Each cadaver lends life to the page. The
arm is a machine, levers rotating on fulcrums, kinesiology
rendered as art. Spread across pages of notebooks, collected in
codices, the idea of man mechanical emerges, a beautiful thing.
One creation following Vetruvian proportion to be liberated
from diagram without the need of patron or political debt, to
escape the woeful technologies of his day, all his art and ardor
shaping each hinged piece. A knight errant to do a genius's
bidding, to sit, to rise, articulated knees and elbows, sinew
adapted to iron. To wave, bow. To move the jaw as if to speak.

In the Anatomical Museum

Bologna, Italy

1.

A gallery of wax figures, medical anomalies captured by Italy's
finest artists in the eighteenth century working from live models
and cadavers. The complete but perforated esophagus of a sword
swallower, sword intact, trachea and lungs attached. A wax bust,
face disfigured by small pox, skin bubbled like oatmeal. A woman
with hydrocephalus, one side of her head normal, the other
monstrously swollen, bald but for a few sprays of auburn hair.
More models than you can bear of infants, twins conjoined at
the crown or side or tailbone. Some premature, some full term.
A model of the genitals of a hermaphrodite. A woman with three
breasts.

2.

In the next gallery, the eye dissected down to its final dark bulb,
petals peeled back, an exotic black flower.

3.

And there, under glass, the full figure of a reclining woman rests
propped against pillows. She is cut open from collar to pubic
bone, extravagantly exposed. Each feature, each organ rendered
with precision, vivid color and detail. A strand of pearls encircles
her wax neck, her expression lovely in its release, head thrown
back, mouth agape as if life were a dream half-remembered,
death a ravishing lover.

Soil Gives Way; Rock Insists

1.
Italian earth exudes. The skin, hands, feet of it. A substance more
human than geological, as much body as it is carbon, calcium,
or iron, made alive by those who tilled and shaped it, fed armies
and empires from it, gave it their battles and blood, built on it,
who have buried themselves, their cities, their artifacts beneath
its crumbled loam. The trees and crops must draw this essence
in, breathe it back into the air, because I do not shake it off, and
the light hums.

2.
In Aquileia beneath the Basilica's marble lies a fine mosaic
floor swept clean, covered over with a plexiglass shield. The first
century tile setters did a bang-up job, their patterns of roosters,
sea monsters, and intricate knots still vivid, and even though I
can't touch it, know what it would feel like to walk on barefoot,
the sound of waves breaking through the villa's open window,
blue shafts of moonlight, the slide of skin against tile cool and
rough that the soles of my feet yearned. The breeze too.

3.
Stone steps lead below that floor to catacombs, a buried pagan
temple converted to a crypt for martyred saints, their bodies
secreted away. Glass-fronted reliquaries preserve their names,
their ulnas and clavicles, a piece of skull. A ring. An undented
silence like the surface of the moon longing for air.

What I Didn't See That Day

The pink marble of the arena at Verona. Not even Verona. Not its lunatics, lovers, or Juliet's balcony. No wish made. Not the Adige. I don't cross it by bridge or boat. No sitting on its bank jotting notes. I don't buy a book of Catallus's poems. Not a fragment. No shop, no church, no castle, no tomb. No great art. No *aperitivo* at an outdoor café. No mango *gelato*. But off the highway before Verona down a bit of a road there is a villa, a dog, an innkeeper, a wine cellar, where the gravel parking area crunches at each step, the little dog barks like a maniac, the innkeeper opens the door, smiles and sets out fresh glasses, and later, the sun still high, you can wander out into the streaming vines.

Lost In

Lisboa

On the terrace I am friends with a purple table, a pink cushion, a circle of shade. The seagulls bark in Portuguese, and the waiter? He must speak English to Americans. He cannot bear to sweep away another broken word. His ears bleed all afternoon. So I am the child softly spoken to, each syllable sweetened, all the spine and arrows smoothed out.

Arrive by 1 pm. No later. He pours my water, says, "Much fresher." Two German men conspire behind me. I am their view, perhaps not spoiled, but imperfect. The wind parts my hair at the back of my head. The umbrellas spin.

The Germans bark too. Now my ears cringe. Give them their beer. They will forget who they are, their complaints dissolve. I will order them more vowels. Below the terrace railing, a whippet with a broken tail noses in the gutter, lifts his leg, disappears around the corner when someone calls.

The soup gone, it is time to play chess with coins. Which is the Queen? Which way out? The waiter holds the umbrella, winks.

To Give, To Get

In Varese my new friend asks me to explain the English word,
"get." *It means too many things—what does this mean, "get?"* She waves
her *Berlitz Dizionario Inglese* at me. It's true. Get this: Get up. Get
over there. Get the news? Get the newspaper. Get the answer.
Get pregnant. Get hungry, thirsty, sick. Get over it. Get in line.
Get there first. Get angry. Get your sister. Get good grades. Get
what you deserve. Get the phone. Get on with it. Get it. Get it?
A guttural clot dislodged from throat to palate-tap, the tongue's
quick contortion to drive the syllable out, get it out. Get decon-
structed, familiarity unraveling. She gets in the front seat, I get
the back.

Souvenir

In a shop on a side street, a cat slept in the window. Tables
held bracelets and rings, beads of glass, stone and metal strung
harmonically. The shopkeeper finished wrapping for a customer
and left me to wander among the objects of beauty and desire,
my last evening in the city. She was a gypsy, a former art student
who excelled in collage, our shared language the composition of
fragments, a careful juxtaposition. Like the art she hung on the
walls. How she tied ribbon on the wrapping. Her black-lined
eyes, shoe-polish hair, smoke-stained teeth. We traded phrases. I
handed her my purchases. She collected my money, the tableaux
as vivid as holding this pen in my hands, untying each word like
a ribbon, letting the bold-colored paper drop to the floor.

Time, Travels

Time and space are modes by which we think, and not conditions in which we live.
—ALBERT EINSTEIN

As the train pulls away, Albert waves at her window, watches until the last car disappears down the track, his time with the woman like a chapter in a book he's been writing. When he lifts the pencil, the ideas don't stop, just as the woman, in her own world, rolls on into her future. Looking back down the track, he sees the past is much the same, a story to wander in memory or bring to life again by writing down. In that way, the past is ever-present. He takes the stairs out of the station into the familiar streets, enjoying the walk, the early evening air, looking forward to getting back to his desk.

* * *

Through the dirty glass he is such a small man on the platform, waving, growing smaller, then gone. As the train gathers speed, she is alone at last with her thoughts. A remarkable person. An unforgettable trip. Once she's home, she'll write down every word.

THREE

Attention, Please

There will be a train in transit at platform 3, a British voice announces.
Last night we ate flying chickens; it's not in the phrase book.
Today I wait for a train, alone, saving a seat for the others on the
bench next to me with our bags. A woman wearing sequined-
toed espadrilles perches at the end. A train is called—I can't be
sure in Italian. Where is everyone? I guard the seat from the
spangled woman's companion who sighs heavily. A train races
past with alarm. The man settles in behind the woman, back
to back. They speak Italian, laugh, relax against each other. The
cheap plastic sound of a water bottle passes between them. I
glance at my watch. No sign of the others. The bushes across the
track lean and whisper. Laundry flaps like semaphores signaling
from the balconies of the houses on the cliffs.

Waves, Cinque Terra

On the shore in Cinque Terra, down the cliff from the trail
between Manarola and Corniglia, even though we have a train
to catch and lodging to secure, we sit down on midnight colored
rocks where the Mediterranean rolls in tumbling them, a rhyth-
mic rush and clatter, rush-clatter. I begin to stack the stones as
high as I can, large to small. My son and his friend strip to their
underwear, dive, swim, the late afternoon sun on water-splash
makes an apparition like silver—they call, beckon me *come in!*
Their bodies, their voices, too, a kind of silver.

How I wanted. How I always will.

I Think of Eugene

Once on a plane headed back home I read a story from one
hundred years ago and sat between men I will never know again.
For a hundred years we spoke of sons and countries, of the arts
that paint us and make us, pages of memory, the unwinding of
time, its approximate realities. One man fell asleep beside me,
that was all, though he remains with me still, a kind of friend
in that he slept so near breathing as my own child might. There
were such kindnesses given in that brief place. I thought of
Eugene, my friend. For some few days we travelled together.
Promises took us other directions. I haven't seen him since. How
can he know how important he became? One seldom will.

"Hai?"... Do You Have?

No *hai*. You leave in the morning. Lunch, a last pasta, then off for
wine, chasing country roads where vines amble among hills green
on green to the edge of the sky. At one cantina, cheese, bread,
salumi served at a farm table. The winemaker shows his cellars,
knows of a job for your son. More wine to pack. A fast drive to the
airport, to sidewalk's cement goodbyes. Nothing stands still. Even
the clouds spin. You check in, pay a $300 extra-baggage charge.

In flight, your husband sleeps. You do not sleep, the ocean, the land
thousands of miles beneath your feet. All that you love.

Family Album III

* * *

1904. Oklahoma territory. Grandpa is five years old. His mother dies in childbirth, but the new brother lives. His father takes Grandpa to visit a family who has no sons. When Grandpa goes to the barn to see the new chicks, his father rides away, never comes back. Grandpa works behind the plow by the time he's eight. "There's nothing sadder," he will one day tell me, "than a motherless child."

* * *

After my mother is born, Grandpa tells Grandma, "Don't let her cry," when he leaves for work each day. "She'll have enough to cry about when she's older." "I didn't let her cry," Grandma later tells me, "but his dinner was never ready."

* * *

Grandma works "from the shoulder down," makes jam and jellies, applesauce, plum sauce, pickles sweet and sour, piccalilli, puts up peaches and apricots, cans tomatoes, shells nuts. Slaughters chickens. Darns socks. During the Depression she sews underwear for my mom and aunt from empty flour sacks. Mom never forgives her, names me after her, and teaches me to sew anyway.

* * *

Perdu Sol

I bring home the ruins. I breathe them in, dream them out,
their dust thick on my tongue. Not the Roman stones or Etrus-
can coins, not the noble relics, but fallen summer palaces, their
rusted trellises, cracked mosaic floors, door frames unhinged and
abandoned to the lizard and the hive or a vine's steady green
grip. What can be pried apart is—left to the wind to crumble
and recollect the seasons' passages, a thousand seasons each filled
with one thousand thousand days and hands that palmed the
once-rock wall to turn a thousand thousand faces to watch the
sea's crimson foil ignite. To watch it fade to turpentine, to ink.
Watch it writing our stories, erasing them, keeping its secret
constant, keeping constant whatever lies cold at the bottom.

Vespers

1.

Almost evening. My car's shadow draws up alongside in the next lane, a companionable presence, reminder that I, too, am something solid even as I pass across the earth at great speed, parting the wind. We shoulder among other shadows for an open stretch of road.

2.

I don't know if it's possible to believe in nothing, but I will try for awhile, escape the clatter of the mind's engine as it struggles to know. And how beautiful is unbelief among the rich and well, the young. In the sun's final moments, earth abandons glory for night's absolution.

3.

Dead poplars etch winter's silhouette into summer's twilight. Dusk ripens, each bird call a crescendo toward silence sad as a remembered lullaby. The sky is bigger than we thought, each thought much bigger than the sky. The swiftening of a bird flashes into night, every shadow swallowed whole.

Finding Time II

To order experience. To avoid a series of obligations. To remember everything we ate. To see the countryside: hike to the hilltop Santuario di San Luca, our son said. Follow the porticoes. So we followed to the outskirts of the fortified city, past the remnant of wall and ancient gate to the Portico di San Luca, climbing uphill, finally up stairs. The basilica crested the outstretched land. We stayed only for the bathroom, a luckless search for a cab back down, the day hot, rolling itself across the sky. But we had the portico, a bottle of water, our desire. Soon, blisters on my feet. The walkway answered every step, the joggers, students, lovers, the tourists with map and book saying *which way now?* Crying, *what more must I see?*

Change of Seasons

That summer I woke up in many rooms to the sound of tides,
awoke to scrub-jay, seagull, or distant traffic, to silence, wind,
and rain, the smell of coffee. Sometimes a blue cupboard,
windows uncurtained where light found its way in. I spoke
only in present tense. I wrote about the past. I never fell asleep
hungry. My suitcases ready, I didn't go to Lisbon, its people
lost to me, but something came ringing its bell-bright sky, a
metropolis of longing on forest trails, the shaded rooms, a crash
of surf. Each day seen first behind closed eyes—I could have been
anywhere—I never knew. The city missing like a lover from my
side, what I thought I was changing in each morning's light in
places I only visited. Everything comes and goes—rooms, cities,
my summers, so far what I know of myself.

Degrees of Separation

Grandpa claims two degrees of separation from Abraham Lincoln who had shaken hands with a young man who much later shakes Grandpa's young hand. "Shake my hand," he'll tell you. "You've just shaken hands with a man who shook hands with a man who shook hands with Abraham Lincoln." I will, many times. Get in line; it can't get better than this. Shake my hand.

Finding Time III

The myth of now. The anticipated sooner becomes the past
where it remains, each moment breached. A son found and lost
again returns as if he had never gone. Where is he now? Going.
Who can tame time? We walked Roman ruins built on Etruscan
stone. A fifth-century chapel stood across from our lodging. We
arrived. We left. The clock on my computer follows a satellite
through its course of stars. The pencil sketches in my journal,
smudged, are carefully dated in black ink. My stemless watch
refuses to have its hands turned back.

"The Book of the Elements of Machines"

Da Vinci's unwritten text

Leonardo recommends gears. Crank, pinion, the toothed wheel
and rack. Also ratchet wheel, pulleys and pulley blocks, axles
of all sorts. To animate the landscape: copy it. Find equilibrium
in a bird's flight. Joints and hinges resemble what they imitate.
Crank to crankshaft. Flywheel. Spring. Study the leg joint, stand
in a far field, use the ten offices of the eye. Cams. Levers of every
kind. Chestnut, elm, oak, and ilex. I am mirror writing with my
left hand. Chains, belts, rotating airscrew, a study of light and
shadow. The unwritten treatise on water. Anatomical aero-
dynamics sketched from a bird's wing. Cantilevers, cadavers.
Cold muscle flayed under the knife. Archetypal geometric forms.
The mental discourse of paint layered image upon image. The
heart is a furnace. It burns air. We will walk on water.

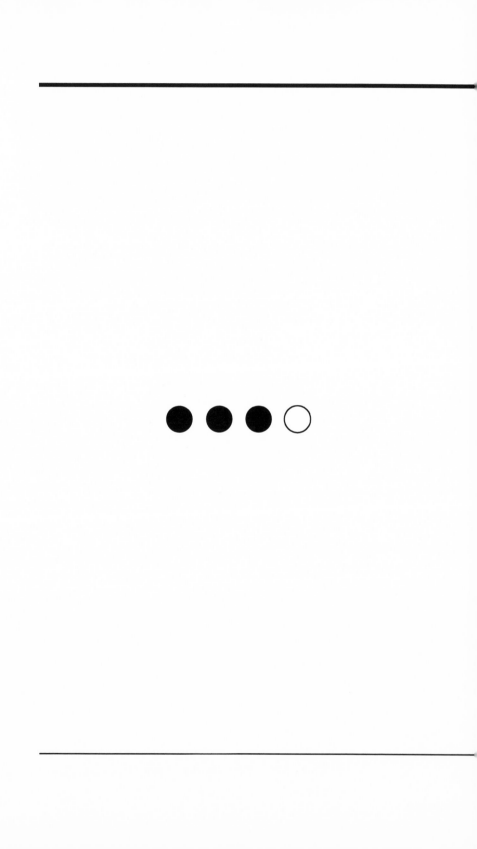

Einstein's Violin II

He wanders from the study to a battered case on the piano
where his violin waits, lifts it out. *Ah, Lina,* the familiar curve
of her polished wooden body fitting against his shoulder.
How inattentive he's been. He pages through sheets of music,
finds Mozart. Already the beloved melody plays in his head, a
symphony rising from the score even before he plays a note, just
the way a mathematical equation scrawled on paper precisely
expresses a thought without words, everything in the cosmos
so elegantly structured. He draws the bow across the A string,
sliding his finger down to middle C, vibrato. It's just a matter of
getting the figures right. Like music.

The note fades, not how light travels, rippling from a billion
light years across space-time, a fabric curved by each star and
planet. Even Newton didn't imagine this invisible geometry, how
it shapes gravity. The sonata unspools from the violin, swells and
dances like gravitational waves. He knows they exist. The
numbers say they must.

The notation quickens. His clumsy fingers fumble. So aggravat-
ing to get old, but it can't be helped. He rests the violin back in
its case, plucks a single string. One pure tone hums, like an idea.
Like the universe finding its voice.

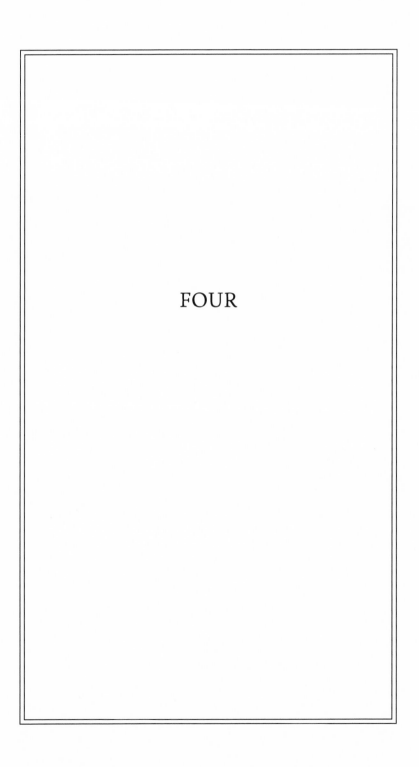

FOUR

And Counting

But when I flew to the moon
it was in a silver Studebaker
the steering wheel like Jupiter's ring
as round as any planet comet streak
constellations dials and gauges
spun so fast it was like standing still
stars whirled past the windshield
I wasn't looking when I saw such things
the sounds I made I cannot make now
I have forgotten how which is why I think
the moon never gets closer than it did then
I knelt on the felted seat holding on
to the steering wheel. And flew.

Eclipse at Solstice

Do you think I could walk pleasantly and well-suited toward annihilation?
—WALT WHITMAN

The moon drew a veil across its face.

I put on my moon-watching socks.

The moon seeking dream peered with one eye, a squint of light.

The moon's memory wiped away.

How like the ancients to howl and be heard, to see Orion's belt and one red star.

To wait for the end, to believe in beginnings, to see that nothing stands still.

And the moon turned red, charred red, and you said it had been 400 years.

Cloud spun thick and covered the sky, the moon's fixed grin, its bloodied face.

To lie on our backs wide open and wait; there is no satisfaction.

I wanted to call everyone; I called to no one but the moon.

And the back door opened and closed.

I felt midnight pass, and the shortest day passed.

And in the moon's dream Walt Whitman, wearing his finest suit, tipped his hat.

The Age of Information

Dusk. Crickets kick in. A frog chorus rises from the creek. Crows have the last word here, and everything finds its place. Time's sweet airs fade forward into the immense where lost planets drift through the Milky Way. We search for them by way of Einstein, by way of desire. We are familiar with dark matter, but vexed by some myth of eternity. What is fourteen billion years? Far out from the edge of evening and our planet's own bending light, a satellite courses. Weightless men consider Mars.

We have never seen so much. We have never been so alone. We have never known so little. It's not, really, so bad.

Revolutions

After sundown, the new moon makes a watermark in the sky, and off to the south a comet leaves a thumbprint of its journey past the planet back to its further orbit in space, time's ancient minutes frozen in a trail of dust and ice. The moon sets, the comet fades, and all is as before. Which is a lie.

I have no proof that Lisbon exists

—FERNANDO PESSOA

only waking dreams, like the cry of a gull
echoing in an alley or the lingering smoke
from a cigarette. Or an imaginary war
that never occurs in your homeland though
everybody bleeds. The idea of Lisbon
is like that, like listening to someone who says
No, then *Yes*, each moment changing direction,
swallows darting mid-sky. And it's summer always
in such a place that can't exist. You walk
on pavement stones slick with heat, the streets
a school of fish flashing through the city
in every direction. They rise under your feet.
This is the dream part, when the trolley turns the corner
shaking like loose change, and the river
opens before you, behind you the hills—a fine
specter, glazed with unerring light.

Saudade, someone might say. Saudade is not
to be alone as I am alone, but to be apart.
Absence is proof of nothing, neither is its phantom pain.
It is a memory stolen from another language
you find you are unable to speak.

Faraway Home

At times I feel jealous—of what I don't know—I want to lie on a
forest floor and cover myself with leaves. I miss my father's face,
I hear my grandmother's voice—singing. And so autumn arrives
in one day while I nap already wearing flannel, some sort of chill
hurrying, the sky cobbled with cloud and desire. Who am I—
longing, hoping for foreign light.

Family Album IV

* * *

1942. Pearl Harbor. My dad spray paints *the japs won't get this scrap arn* on his old Model T Ford to drive in a local parade. He enlists in the Air Force, works as a radio operator in the Philippines, contracts TB, is honorably discharged. Back home he attends college, excels in debate, and hopes to become a lawyer, but his mother tells him it's better to go to work instead. He takes a sales job, drops out.

* * *

My dad enlists his German Shepherd, Mike, to serve in the canine patrol of the US Army. Mike also receives an honorable discharge, though details of his service remain an Army secret. The next Fourth of July, Mike tries to claw his way up the chimney when the fireworks begin.

* * *

My mother could have been a doctor. As a child, she and a friend trap neighborhood tomcats, etherize them, and perform successful neutering in a shed. Yes, she sews them up. *They didn't seem to mind*, she will say. Later she works with a country doctor attending home births of destitute women. She meets my dad her first year of college, marries him instead.

* * *

We're Traveling

Redwing blackbirds perch in mustard plants, and the first rain-
drops hit the windshield. It's weird in this bumpy car to stare
out the window at everything that rushes past. At everything
that stands completely still while I rush past, the pavement wet
and glistening now, the rain falling hard. My husband drives.
We don't talk. We travel together separate journeys; who knows
what he sees. We pass the oil refinery; the rain tapers off. The
tires play a rhythm across the bridge, its rusted fretwork raised
above an empty train yard. The Navy's mothball fleet sits like
game pieces, the water gray leather. I am watching and do not
mind the traffic closed in on all sides. The car moves in and out
guided by small adjustments I don't control. I hand five dollars
to my husband at the toll booth, happy at the taste of cool air
through his window, glad to be warm when the window slides
closed. I've come this way so many times, familiar with the
scenery. How the hand of different seasons works upon it, and
how the hands of farmers have their way. Where the fields lie
fallow for a season, and when a field is given up for houses, and
how the strip malls tie them close together. It's difficult to speak
these things to anyone, the gratitude I feel to pass each land-
mark, to be swallowed up in memory and motion, to see light
strike the hills aslant and strange. To hear the redwing blackbird
cry in summer. To watch a hawk reel, dive.

Home

My grandfather would have sized up this crowd with two words: *local yokels.*

When a stranger moves to town we call him *immigrant.*

If we move to a foreign country we call ourselves *ex-pats* instead.

To travel from one place to another we lock our houses first.

To dream, the mind throws the doors open wide.

Either way we leave what we know behind.

To know ourselves better we've unlocked the genome.

We discover we're related to everyone everywhere.

We're also made of star stuff blown from the corners of the cosmos.

Therefore wherever we wander we're home.

Follow the Tail Lights

Trees close in, billboards announce the next town's fast-food
stops. Half-empty parking lots. Peaches, plums for sale,
regimented corn.

A hermit barn crouches, sorghum tassels gleam. An oak's long
shadow follows profound textures of change. What will stand,
what turns under? The heron's black feet trail, rudder it over the
freeway, a rest stop, a rice field; its white wings beat slow, the
way a woman fans herself in church. Pews full of alfalfa. I don't
pull over, the road irresistible, the windows for once rolled down
all the way.

How to Wind a Watch

Now another installment of time opens.
—JULIO CORTÁZAR

First you must. Do not be afraid to assist. Take it in your hands,
a little wheel for turning pinched. Finger and thumb. The pitch
and yaw a simple, obsolete technology you will never forget.
The wheel is on a stem. The stem cannot be plucked. Pull, and
move the hands of time. It is not absolute, you must remember.
Motion affects the intervals. Go back in time. Manipulate its
mechanics. Hand is the root of manipulate. Hand me the watch.

I'll do it.

ACKNOWLEDGEMENTS

Thanks to those who encouraged this text at various stages: Mary Donnelly, Kelsea Habecker, Marjorie Manwaring, Nils Peterson, Dean Rader, Jennifer K. Sweeney, and Ann Dernier.

Many thanks to Glenn Patterson for choosing "A Theory of Relativity" as first prize in the Fish Flash Fiction Prize.

My deep appreciation to the Lucas Artists Residency Program at Montalvo Arts Center for the gift of Time and amazing Space to work on the manuscript, and especially to director Kelly Sicat.

I owe gratitude to both Stefan Moeller and Rolf Laessig, two physicist friends, as well as to PBS's *Science Friday* with host Ira Flato, who keep my interest fueled and my understanding reasonably on track. *Danke schön.*

Special thanks to editor Marci Johnson whose interest in *The Behaviour of Clocks* since a first conversation at AWP finally brought the book to publication at WordFarm, and for Sally and Andrew Craft, publishers, who so warmly received it there.

Thanks in all ways to Frank Ashton.

Grateful acknowledgements to the following publications where pieces, sometimes in slightly different form, first appeared: *ANMLY* (FKA *Drunken Boat*), *Best American Poetry Blog, Caesura, Fish Anthology 2014*, First Prize, *Hinchas de Poesia, Local Habitations*: Laurel Editions, *Map Literary, Poet Lore, Poetry Flash, Red Wheelbarrow, Sandhill Review, Some Odd Afternoon*: BlazeVOX, *sparkle&blink, Spoon River Poetry Review, The Wax Paper, Zyzzyva.*

DEDICATIONS

"Family Album I" in memory of Ebba Fredrika Stockard.

"Some Birth Day" after Dylan Thomas.

"Side Trip" for Pio Costantini.

"Gratitude" for Mara Masutti.

"My planet is making me dizzy" for Susannah Ashton.

"In the Rain, Udine," *Albergo Ristorante Costantini*, Tarcento, Italy.

"In the Anatomical Museum," *Museo delle Cere Anatomiche*, Bologna, Italy.

"Lost In" for the restaurant, Lisbon, Portugal.

"Finding Time II" for James Ashton.

"Faraway Home" for Marta Bonito.

"To Give, To Get" for Paola Cinquepalmi.

"And Counting" in memory of Caswell M. Stockard, Jr.

"Degrees of Separation" in memory of William V. Welch.

"Home" for Nils Peterson.

"Follow the Tail Lights" for Alan Soldofsky.

ABOUT THE AUTHOR

Sally Ashton is editor-in-chief of *DMQ Review*, an online journal featuring poetry and art. Writing across genres, in collaboration with artists, and specializing in short prose forms, Ashton is the author of three collections, *Some Odd Afternoon, Her Name Is Juanita,* and *These Metallic Days,* and she is assistant editor of *They Said: A Multi-Genre Anthology of Contemporary Collaborative Writing.* She has taught at San José State University, UC Santa Cruz Extension, and workshops including *Disquiet: International Literary Program* in Lisbon, Portugal. She served as Santa Clara County's Poet Laureate, 2011-2013. Other honors include fellowships from Arts Council Silicon Valley and a Lucas Artist Residency at Montalvo Arts Center. She lives in California with her husband.